Varney

HOLD THE ANCHOVIES!

A BOOK ABOUT PIZZA

Written by

Shelley Rotner & Julia Pemberton Hellums

Photographs by Shelley Rotner

Orchard Books

New York

Most everybody likes pizza.

What is pizza made of?

Pizza is made from many things. The first is dough. In order to make pizza dough, we need flour.

Flour is made from ground-up kernels of wheat.

The dough is made by adding warm water and yeast to the flour.

Some cooks add olive oil to make the crust crispy.

The yeast is what makes

the dough rise, or grow bigger.

We knead the dough by folding and pushing it with the palms of our hands.

This makes the dough really stretch.

When the dough rises
and stretches just
the right amount,
it is ready to be
tossed into the shape
of a pizza pie.

**The next thing we need is sauce
made from sweet, ripe tomatoes.**

Tomatoes need sun, clean water, and good soil to grow.

To make sauce, the tomatoes need to be chopped and cooked.

Spices and herbs add more flavor. The sauce is spread evenly on the dough.

Now comes the cheese.
We'll use mozzarella, made with cow's milk.

Milk is mixed with an ingredient called rennet, which causes it to thicken. The mixture is heated until it thickens even more and turns into curds. Curds are pressed into balls of cheese.

The cheese is grated and sprinkled onto the pizza.

Peppers need the same conditions as tomatoes to grow.

Mushrooms are different. They grow best in dark, wet places.

Pepperoni is chewy, peppery meat made from pigs.

Anchovies are small, silvery fish. A lot of people don't like them on their pizza. Yuck! Hold the anchovies!

Now everything is ready to go into the oven. Heat is what makes the pizza cook.

The dough turns crisp and brown, the sauce bubbles, and the cheese melts. Mmm, we can smell the pizza cooking.

And it tastes good too!

BASIC PIZZA RECIPE

Ingredients

Pizza Dough:

1	package (1/4 ounce) rapid-rise yeast
1/2	teaspoon sugar
1/2	cup lukewarm water (105° to 115°F)
1 1/2	cups all-purpose flour, unsifted
1/2	teaspoon salt
1 1/2	teaspoons olive oil, plus some extra oil for bowl and pan
1/2	cup prepared tomato sauce
1 1/2	cups (6 ounces) grated mozzarella cheese
1/2	cup mushrooms, pepperoni, peppers, or toppings of your choice

Preparation

1. Dissolve yeast and sugar in water; let stand 2 minutes, until bubbles form.
2. Place flour and salt in a medium-size bowl. Make a small well in the center of the flour.
3. Pour dissolved yeast into the well. Gradually mix the flour from the edges of the well into the yeast, using a wooden spoon. Mix well. Stir in olive oil.
4. Place dough on a lightly floured wooden board and knead it by using a pushing and folding motion for about 1 to 2 minutes, until dough is smooth and elastic.
5. Place dough in an oiled bowl. Brush some oil over the top of dough. Cover bowl and allow dough to rise in a warm place for 15 to 20 minutes, until it doubles in size.
6. Preheat oven to 450°F. Prepare topping(s). Lightly oil a 12-inch pizza plate.
7. Press dough into oiled pan. Prick with fork.
8. Spoon tomato sauce onto the dough and spread it evenly.
9. Sprinkle cheese evenly over the tomato sauce. Add your choice of topping(s).
10. Bake in oven 15 to 20 minutes, until cheese is melted and crust is lightly browned.

Orchard Books
95 Madison Avenue
New York, NY 10016

Manufactured in Singapore
Printed by Toppan Printing Company, Inc.
Photographs of pizza boxes by Lightworks Photographic
Book design by Hans Teensma/Impress, Inc.

10 9 8 7 6 5 4 3 2 1

Library of Congress Cataloging-in-Publication Data
Rotner, Shelley.
Hold the anchovies! : a book about pizza / written
by Shelley Rotner and Julia Pemberton Hellums ;
photographs by Shelley Rotner.
p.   cm.
Summary: Describes the ingredients that are
used to make a pizza, where each comes from, and how
they are used to prepare final product. Includes recipe.
ISBN 0-531-09507-X.
ISBN 0-531-08857-X (lib. bdg.)
1. Pizza—Juvenile literature. 2. Pizza—Pictorial
works—Juvenile literature.   [1. Pizza.
2. Cookery.]   I. Title.
TX770.P58R67 1996
641.8'24—dc20   96-3999